Cursive Writing
for Adults

Table of Contents

Introduction……………………………………………………………03

The rules of Writing…………………………………………………04

Level One: Letters and words …………………………………06

Level Two: Quotes, Write with me……………………………84

Level Three: Quotes, Self-Writing ……………………………118

Introduction

Luckily, improving your handwriting does not require months of learning. The following book will help you to quickly find your flow again. With writing letters, words and poems, your level improves every day. This Complete Cursive Writing book teaches you How to improve your current Handwriting to a Beautiful and Legible Cursive Handwriting. if you want to improve your writing even further, you will need to practice. Going through this handwriting pages will get you to practice your handwriting on a daily basis until you perfect it.

Benefits to writing by hand

One study found that students who take notes longhand are able to better retain the information, compared to those who type out notes using a laptop. When typing out notes, students tended to simply take verbatim notes. However, when writing out notes by hand, you engage your brain, which has a positive impact on your ability to remember the material. Not only does this improve your memory, but it also gives you a better grasp on the subject, as you are not merely mindlessly processing the information.

Time

Flexible Timings, You can do it in your free time of the day. Every day you need 30 to 45 mins, depending on your skills and speed.

The rules of writing
Uppercase Cursive Alphabet

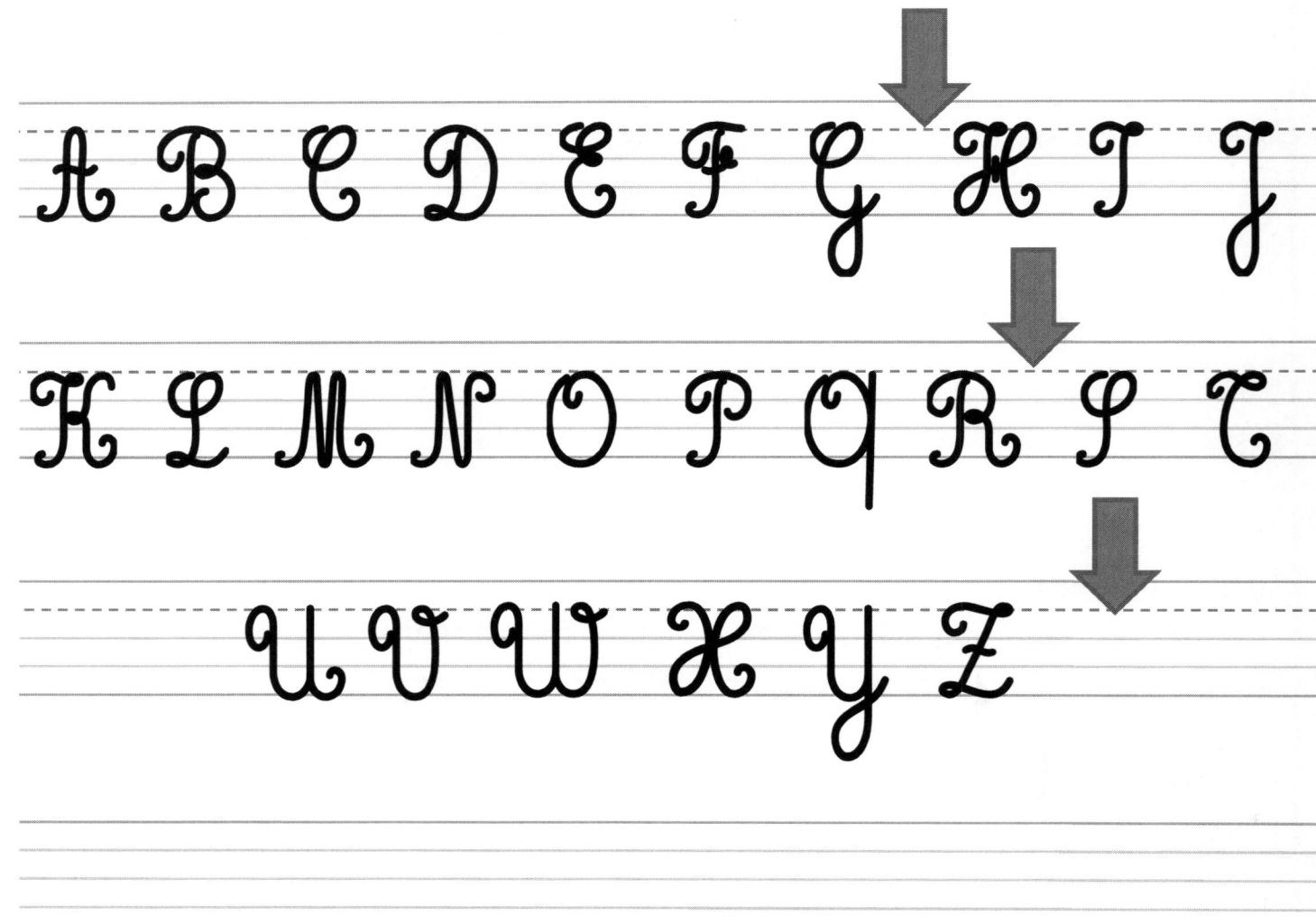

The rules of Writing
Lowercase Cursive Alphabet

5

𝒜 𝒜 𝒜 𝒜 𝒜 𝒜

𝒜 𝒜 𝒜 𝒜 𝒜 𝒜

𝒜 𝒜 𝒜 𝒜 𝒜 𝒜

𝒜

𝒜

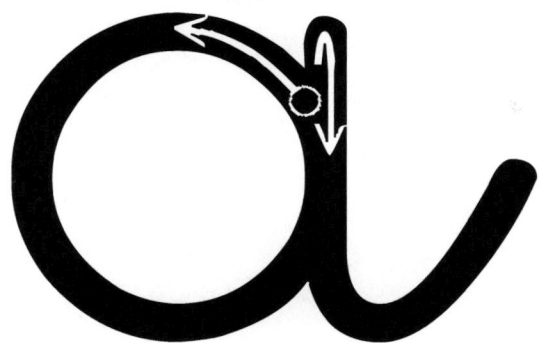

a a a a a a

a a a a a a

a a a a a a

a

a

aeroplane   aeroplane
aeroplane   aeroplane
aeroplane
aeroplane

armchair   armchair   armchair
armchair
armchair

aeroplane

armchair

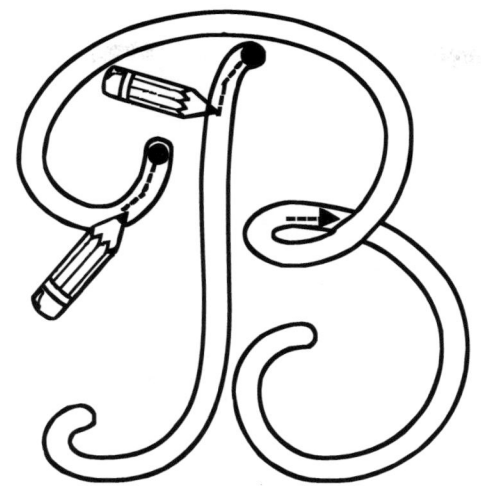

𝓑 𝓑 𝓑 𝓑 𝓑 𝓑

𝓑 𝓑 𝓑 𝓑 𝓑 𝓑

𝓑 𝓑 𝓑 𝓑 𝓑 𝓑

𝓑

𝓑

9

barber *barber barber barber*
barber barber
barber barber
barber barber

baby *baby baby baby*
baby baby
baby baby
baby baby

barber

baby

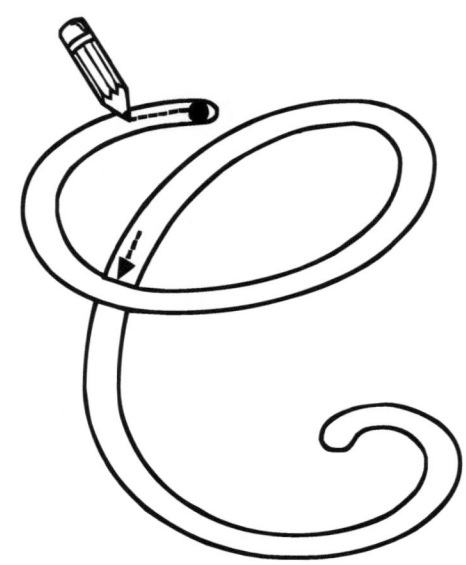

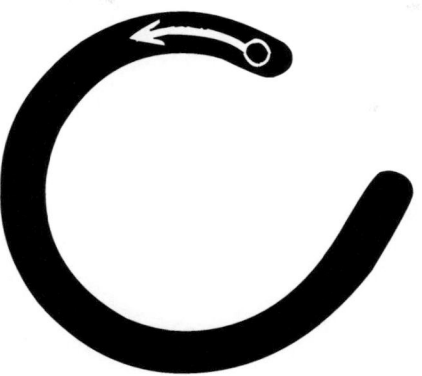

c c c c c c c

c c c c c c c

c c c c c c

c

c

cat   cat   cat   cat   cat
cat   cat
cat   cat
cat   cat

racket   racket   racket   racket
racket   racket
racket   racket
racket   racket

cat

racket

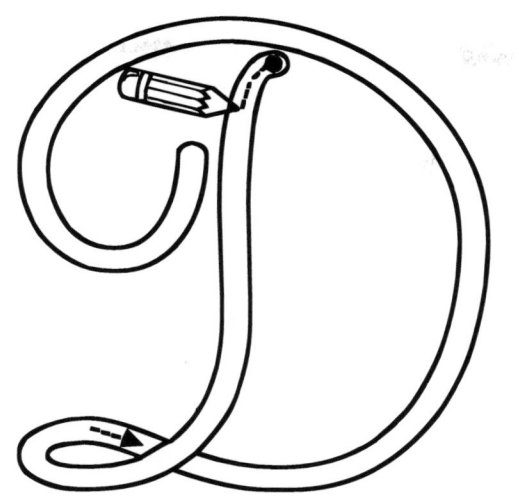

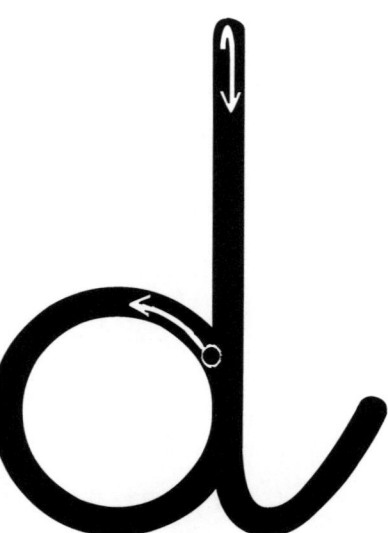

d   d   d   d   d   d

d   d   d   d   d   d

d   d   d   d   d

d

d

domino domino domino
domino domino
domino domino
domino domino

shed shed shed shed shed
shed shed
shed shed
shed shed

domino

shed

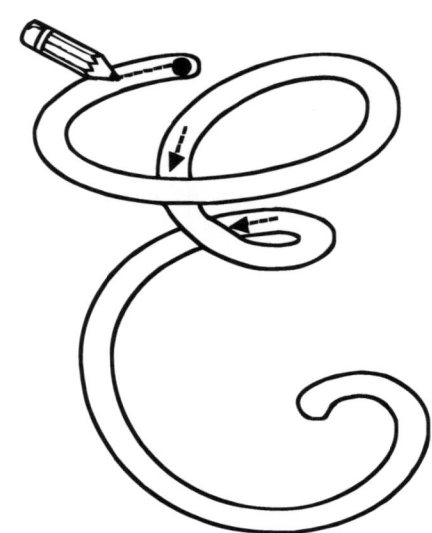

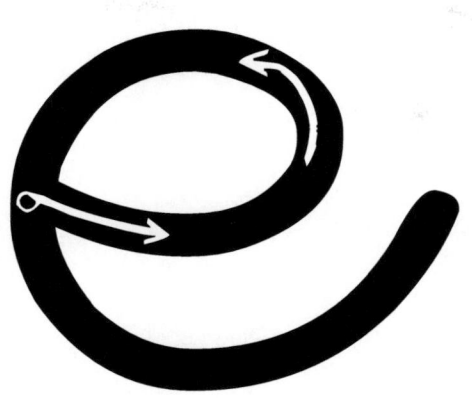

e e e e e e

e e e e e e

e e e e e

e

e

eight   *eight*   *eight*   *eight*
eight   *eight*
eight   *eight*
eight   *eight*

sweet   *sweet*
sweet   *sweet*   *sweet*   *sweet*
sweet   *sweet*
sweet   *sweet*

eight

sweet

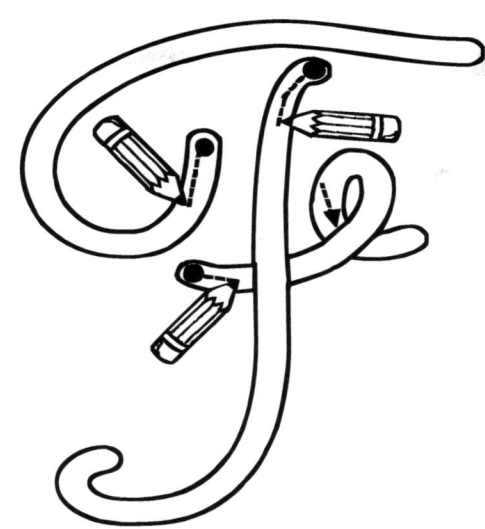

21

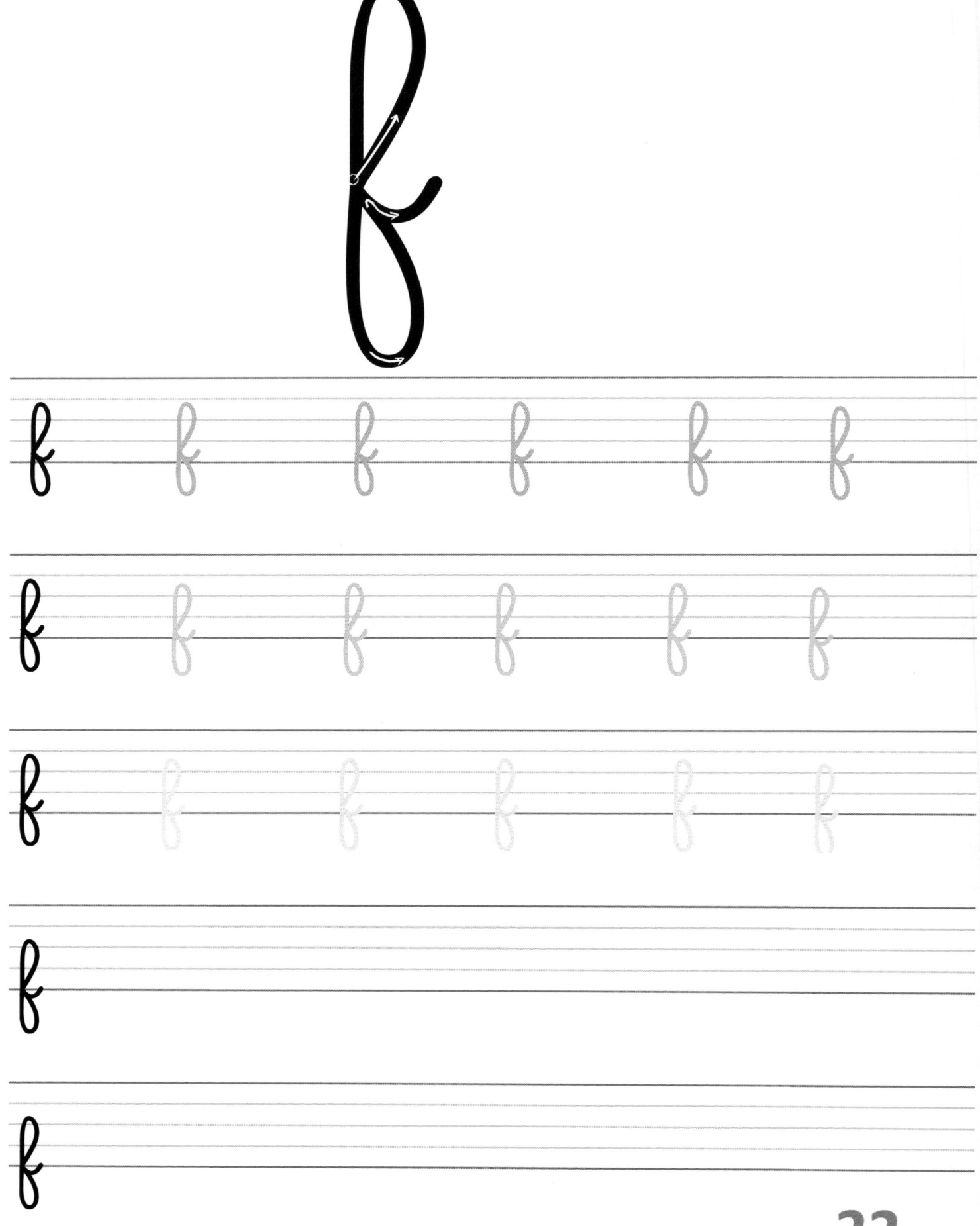

22

fish fish fish fish fish
fish fish
fish fish
fish fish

starfish starfish starfish starfish
starfish starfish
starfish starfish
starfish starfish

fish

starfish

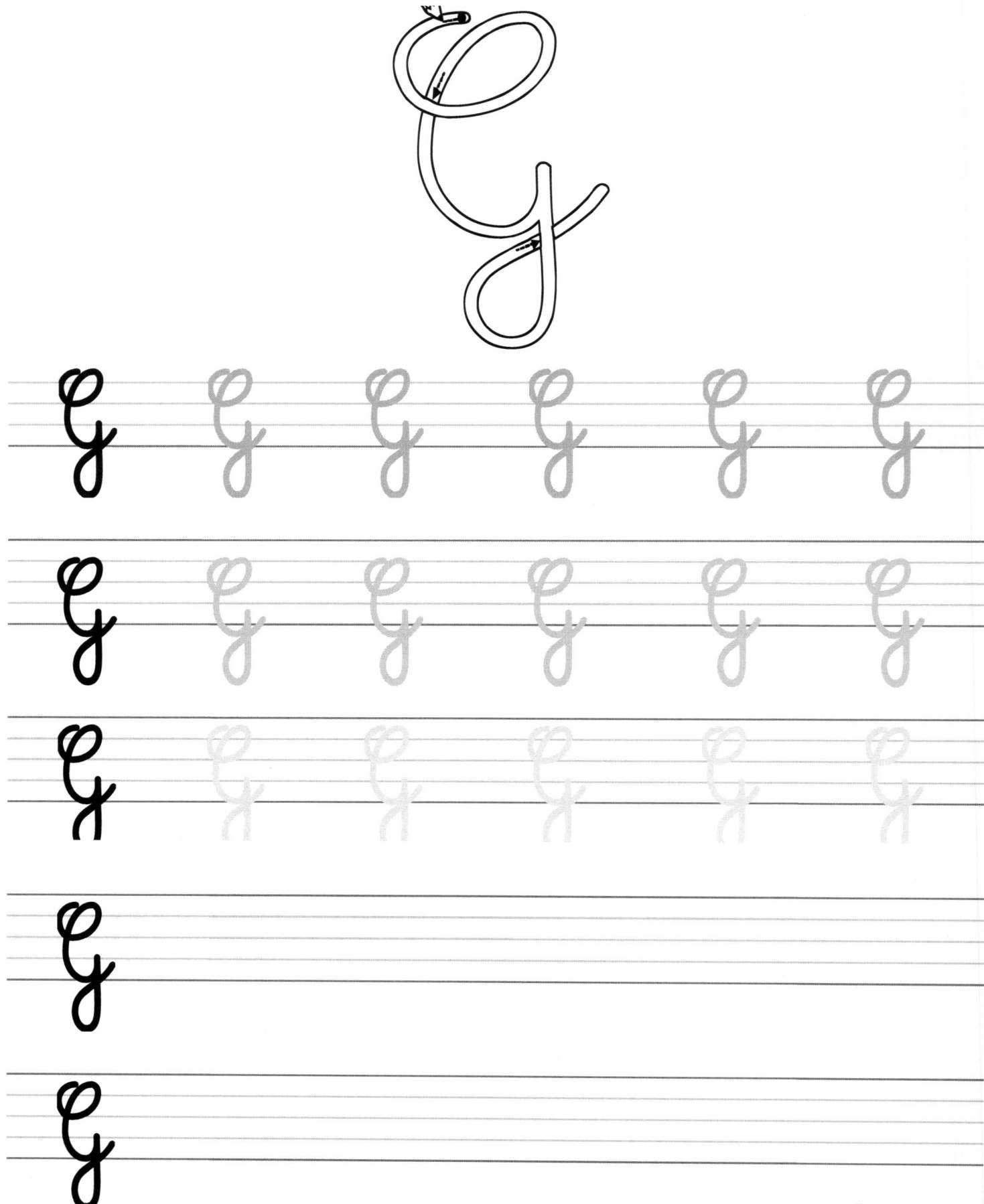

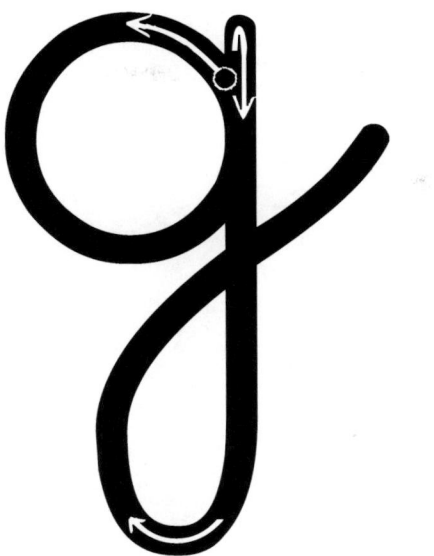

g g g g g g

g g g g g g

g g g g g

g

g

glasses glasses glasses glasses
glasses glasses
glasses glasses
glasses glasses

tiger tiger tiger tiger tiger
tiger tiger
tiger tiger
tiger tiger

glasses

tiger

27

h h h h h h

h h h h h h

h h h h h h

h

h

horse horse horse horse horse
horse horse
horse horse
horse horse

match match match match match
match match
match match
match match

horse

match

T T T T T T

T T T T T T

T T T T T T

T

T

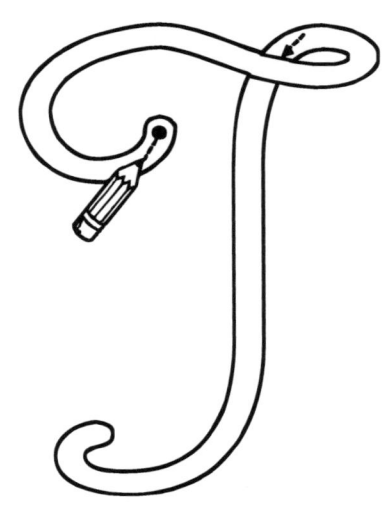

i i i i i i

i i i i i i

i i i i i i

i

i

igloo igloo igloo igloo igloo
igloo igloo
igloo igloo
igloo igloo

girl girl girl girl girl girl
girl girl
girl girl
girl girl

igloo

girl

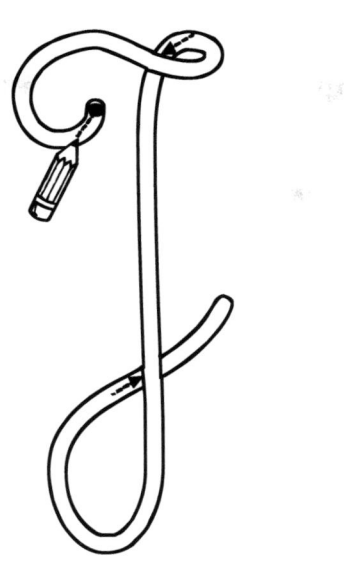

33

34

judge judge judge judge judge
judge judge
judge judge
judge judge

pyjamas pyjamas pyjamas pyjamas
pyjamas pyjamas
pyjamas pyjamas
pyjamas pyjamas

judge

pyjamas

36

k

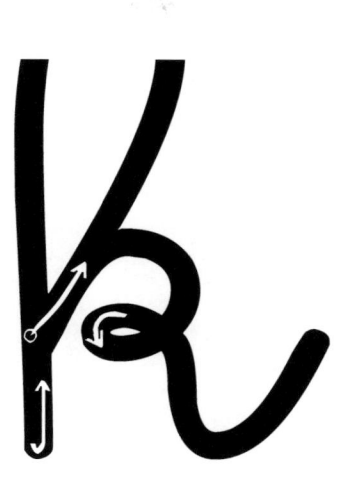

k k k k k k

k k k k k k

k k k k k

k

k

karate karate karate karate
karate karate
karate karate
karate karate

kiwi kiwi kiwi kiwi kiwi kiwi
kiwi kiwi
kiwi kiwi
kiwi kiwi

karate

kiwi

39

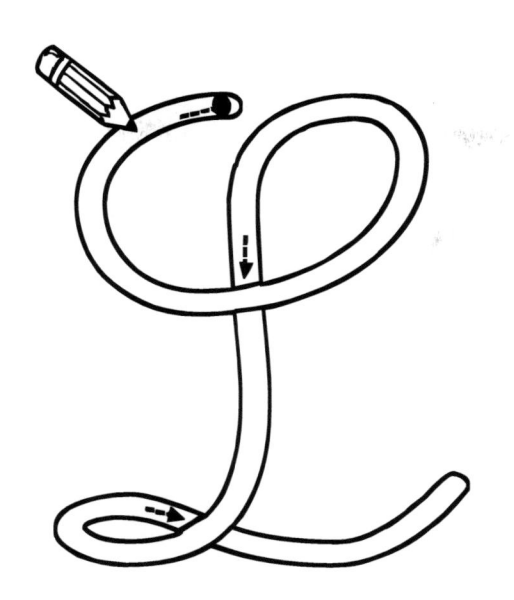

ℓ   ℓ   ℓ   ℓ   ℓ   ℓ   ℓ

ℓ   ℓ   ℓ   ℓ   ℓ   ℓ   ℓ

ℓ   ℓ   ℓ   ℓ   ℓ   ℓ   ℓ

ℓ

ℓ

lion lion lion lion lion lion
lion lion
lion lion
lion lion

seal seal seal seal seal seal
seal seal
seal seal
seal seal

lion

seal

M

m

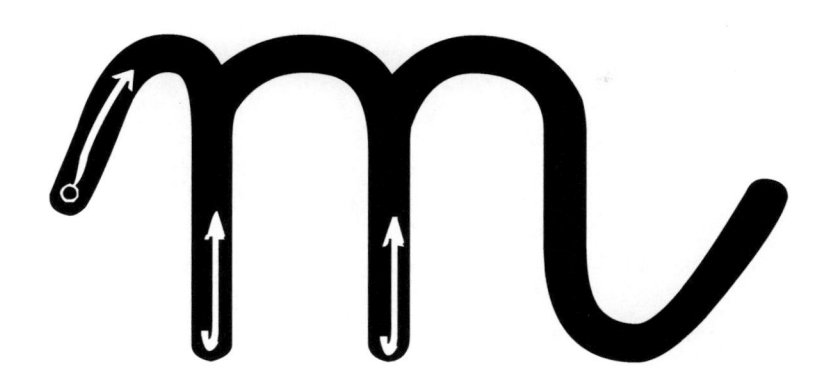

mermaid   mermaid   mermaid

mermaid   mermaid

mermaid   mermaid

mermaid   mermaid

hammer   hammer   hammer

hammer hammer

hammer hammer

hammer hammer

mermaid

hammer

45

n

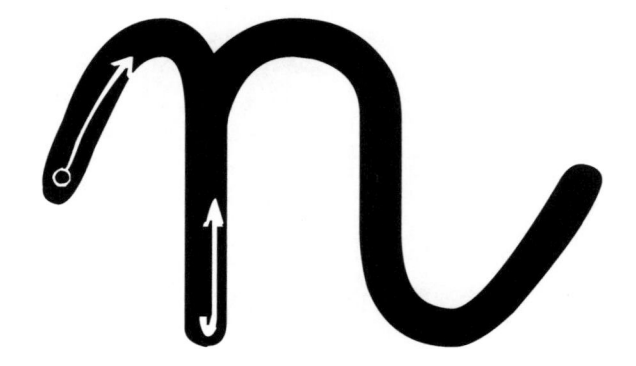

n   n   n   n   n   n

n   n   n   n   n   n

n   n   n   n   n   n

n

n

nest nest nest nest nest nest
nest nest
nest nest
nest nest

banana banana banana banana
banana banana
banana banana
banana banana

nest

banana

47

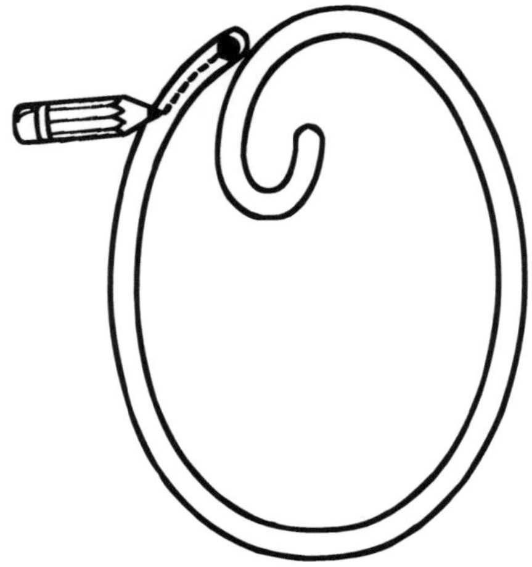

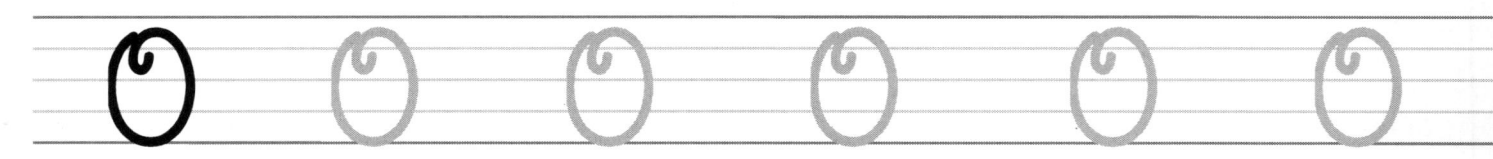

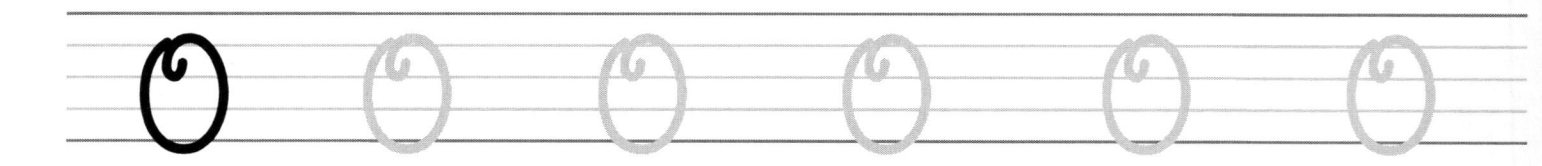

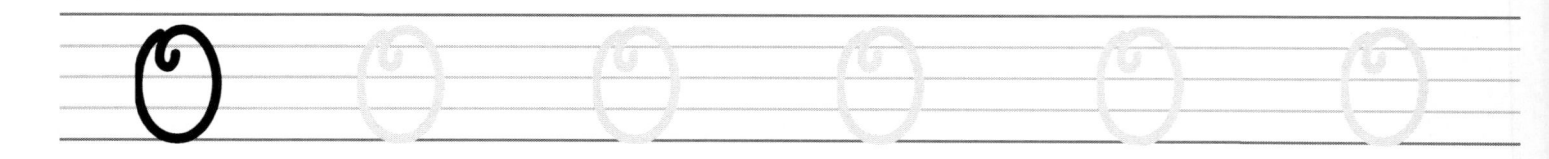

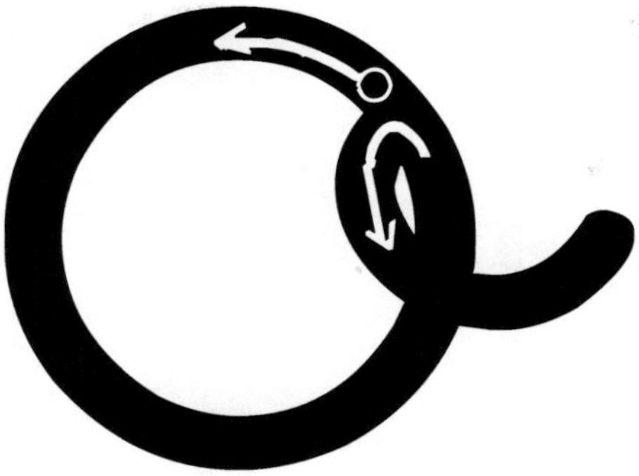

orange orange orange orange
orange orange
orange orange
orange orange

school school school school
school school
school school
school school

orange

school

51

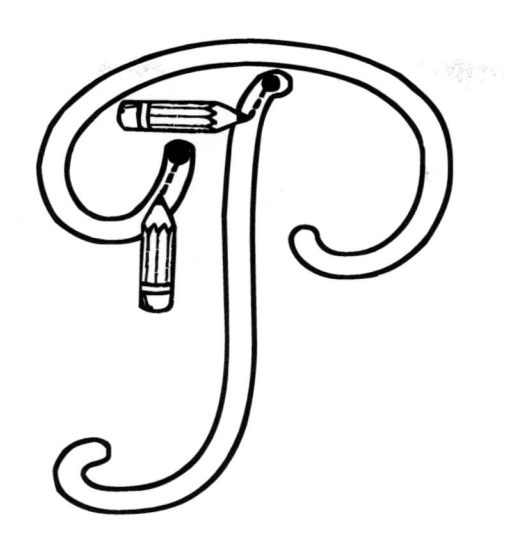

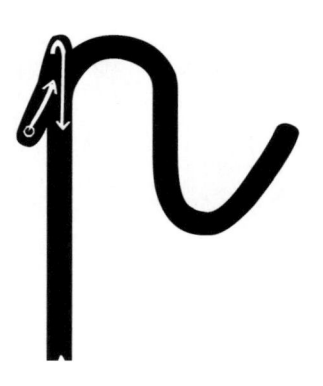

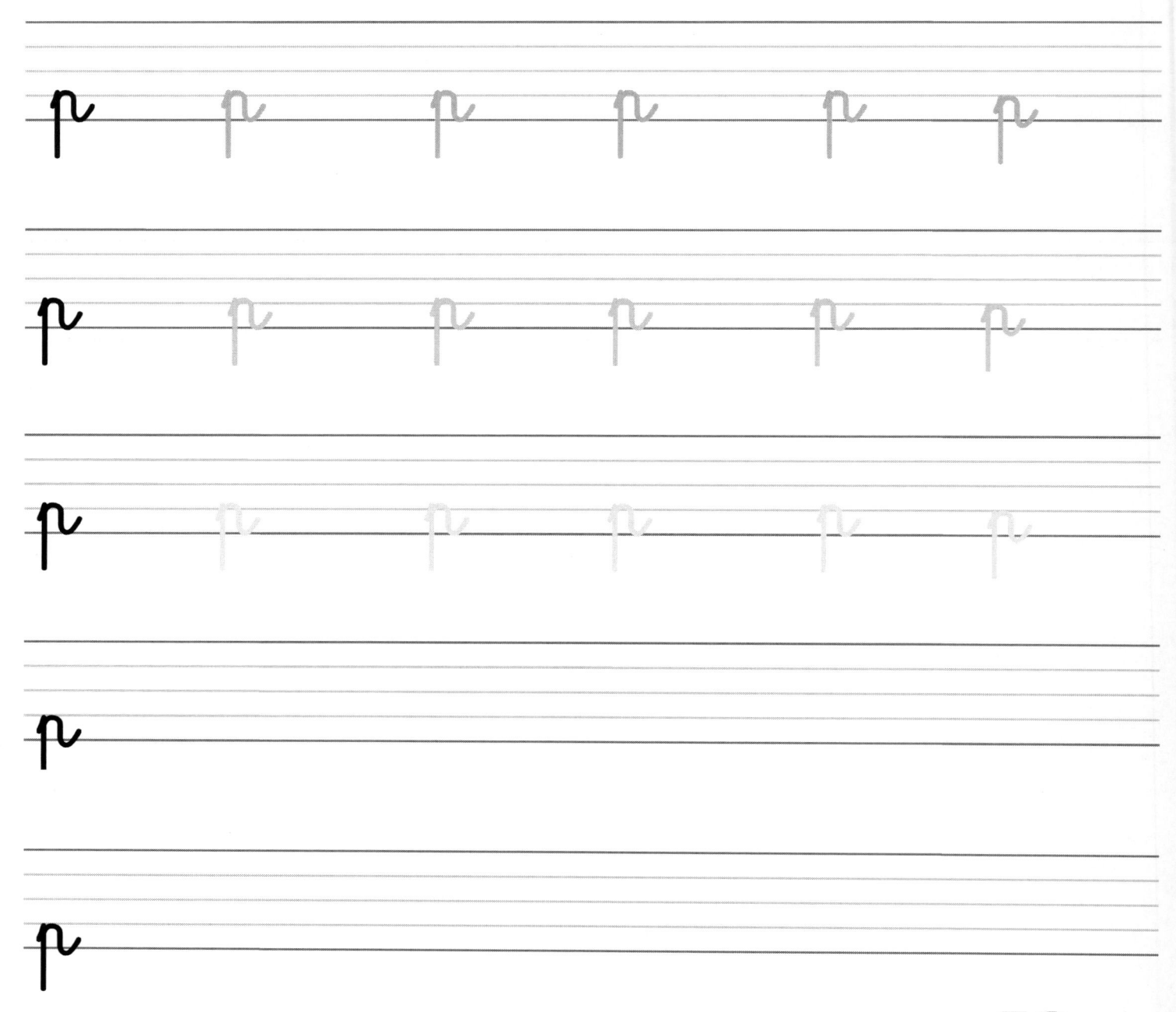

pear   pear   pear   pear   pear
pear   pear
pear   pear
pear   pear

pirate   pirate   pirate   pirate
pirate   pirate
pirate   pirate
pirate   pirate

pear

pirate

53

54

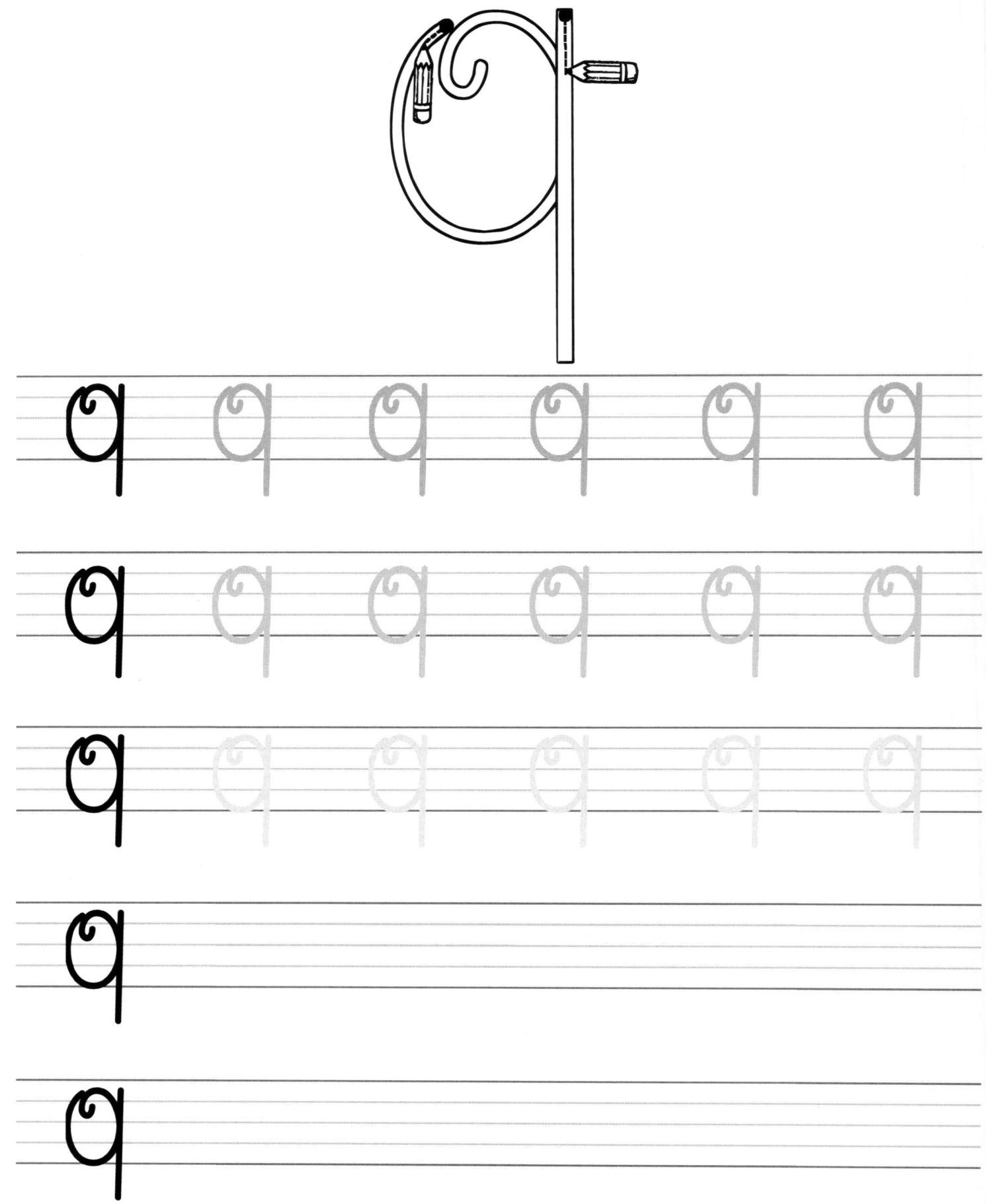

q

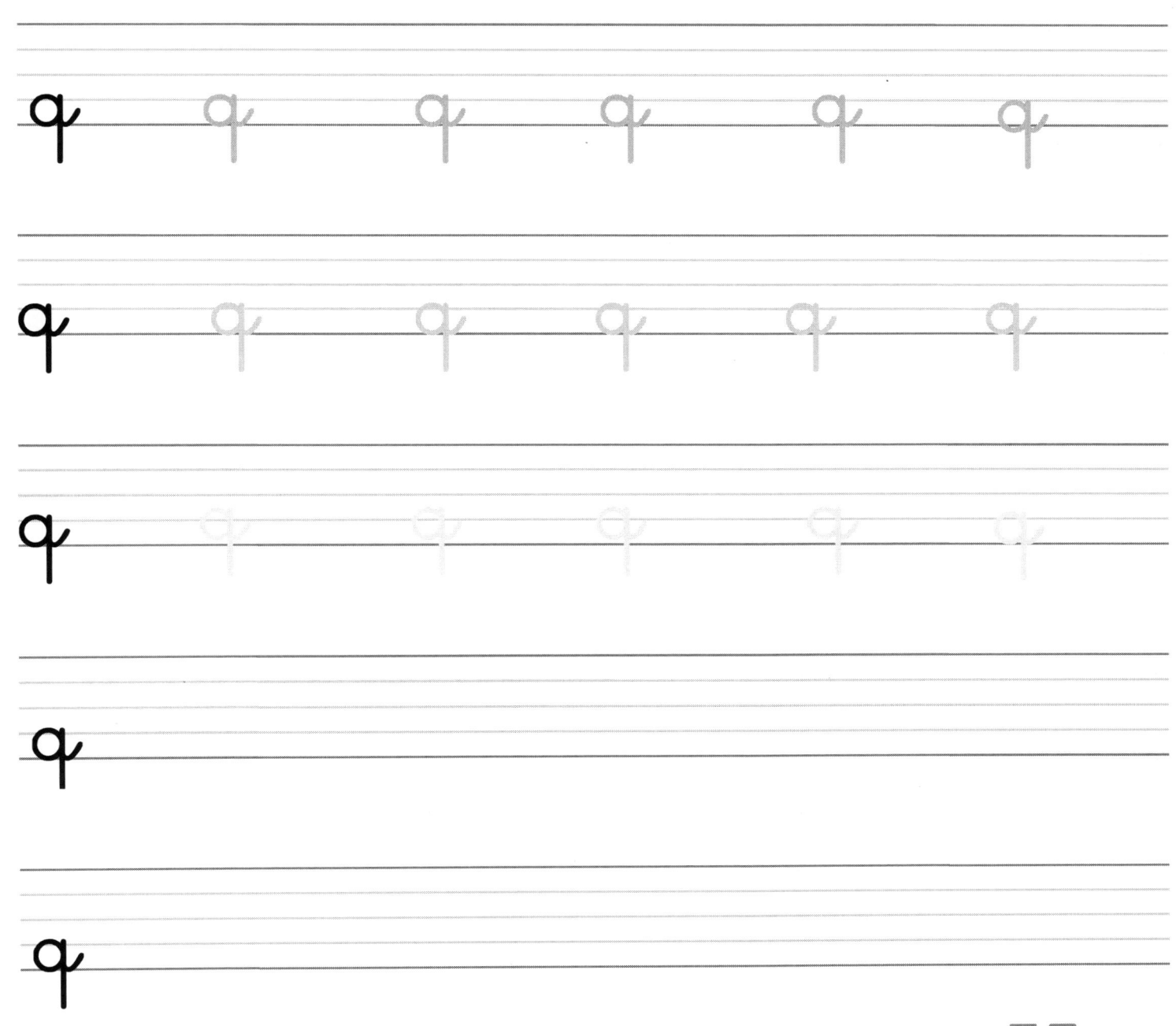

55

queen queen queen queen queen
queen queen
queen queen
queen queen

oaq oaq oaq oaq oaq oaq
oaq oaq
oaq oaq
oaq oaq

queen

oaq

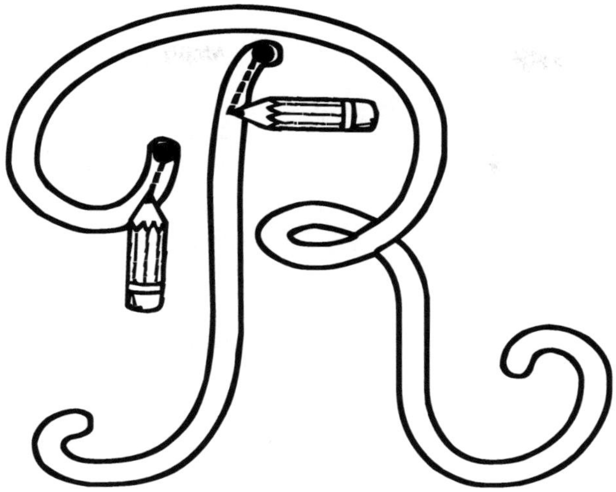

R R R R R R

R R R R R R

R R R R R R

R

R

58

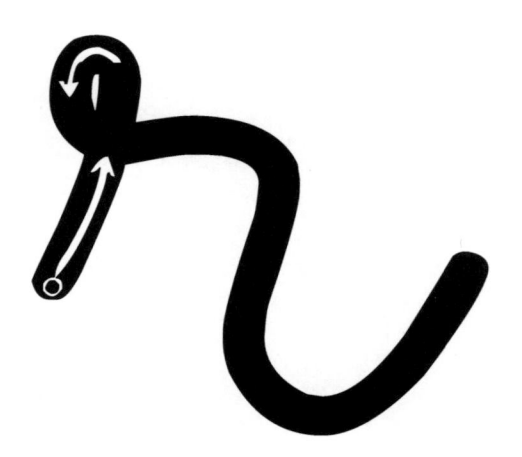

rabbit   rabbit   rabbit   rabbit   rabbit

rabbit   rabbit

rabbit   rabbit

rabbit   rabbit

parrot   parrot   parrot   parrot

parrot   parrot

parrot   parrot

parrot   parrot

rabbit

parrot

60

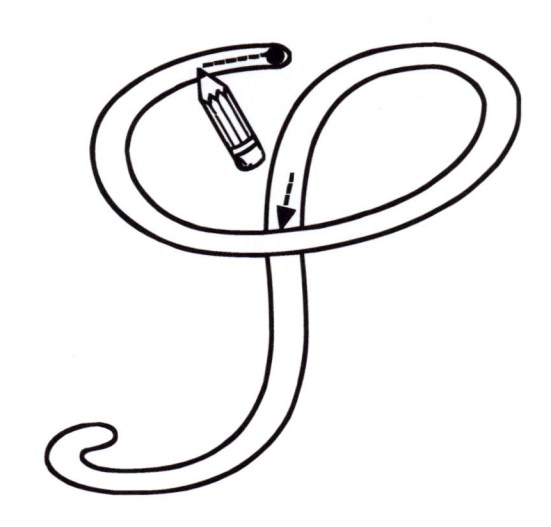

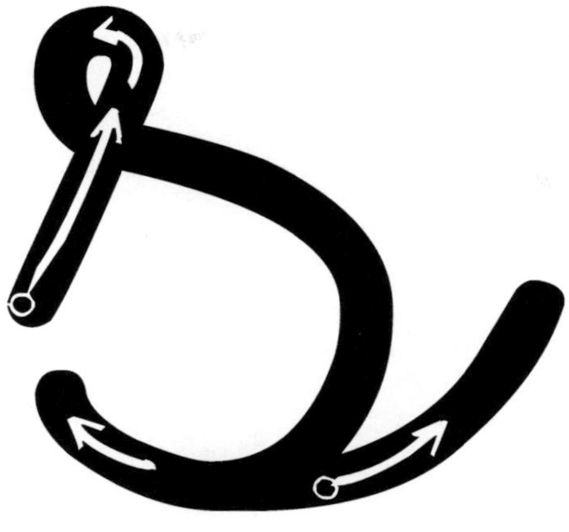

scorpion   scorpion   scorpion
scorpion   scorpion
scorpion   scorpion
scorpion   scorpion

dress   dress   dress   dress
dress   dress
dress   dress
dress   dress

scorpion

dress

63

t

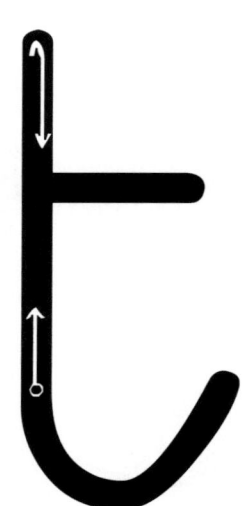

tortoise tortoise tortoise tortoise
tortoise tortoise
tortoise tortoise
tortoise tortoise

raft raft raft raft raft raft
raft raft
raft raft
raft raft

tortoise

raft

Ու

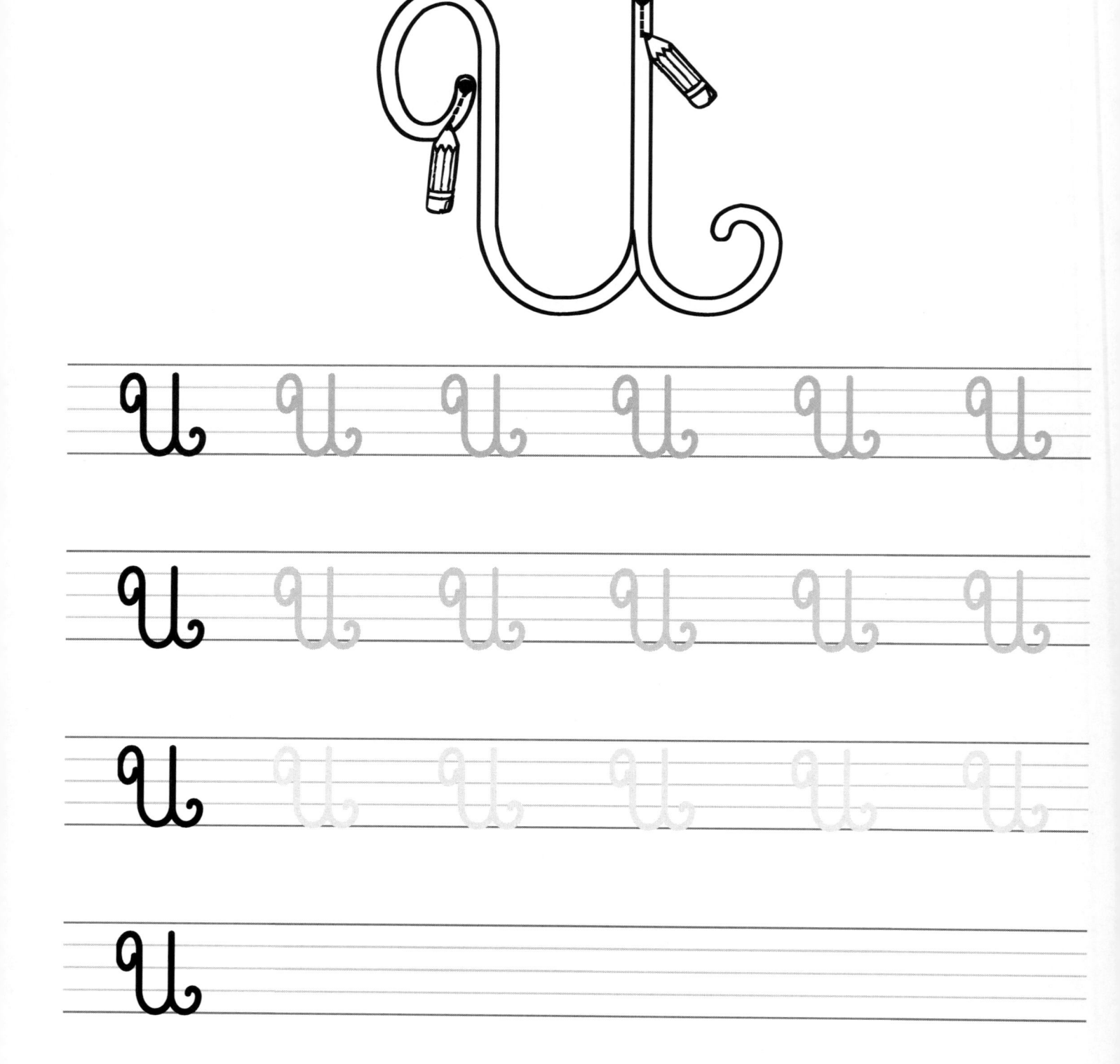

u

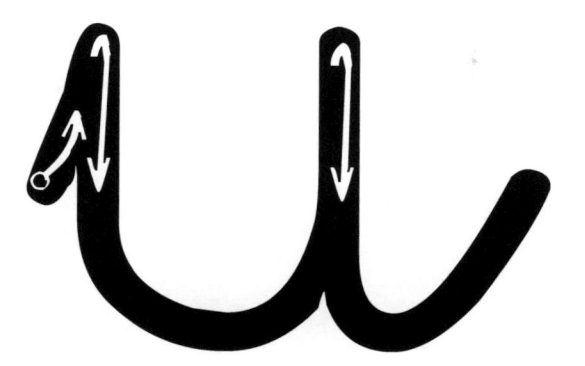

unicorn   unicorn   unicorn   unicorn
unicorn   unicorn
unicorn   unicorn
unicorn   unicorn

guitar   guitar   guitar   guitar
guitar   guitar
guitar   guitar
guitar   guitar

unicorn

guitar

69

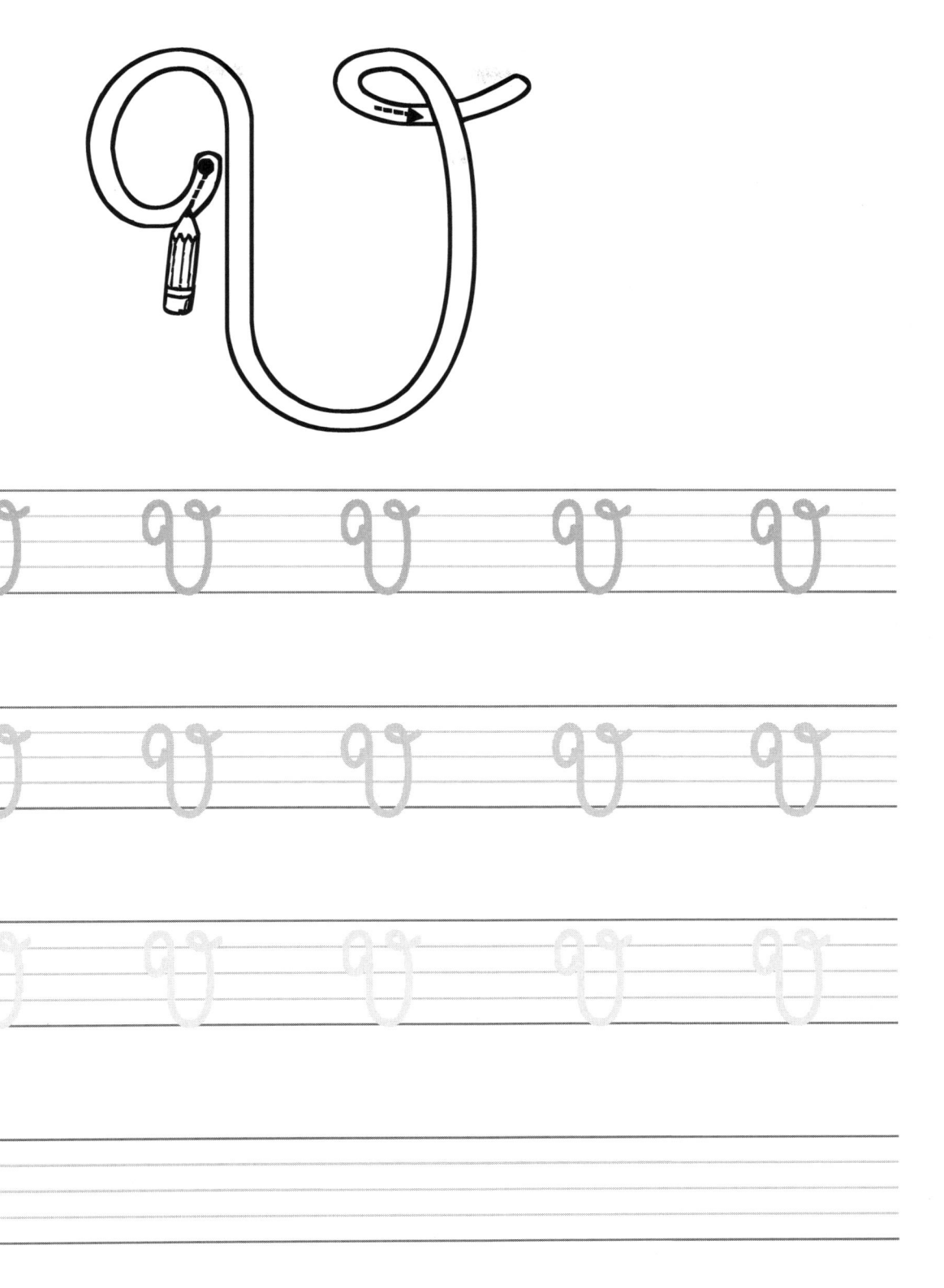

v

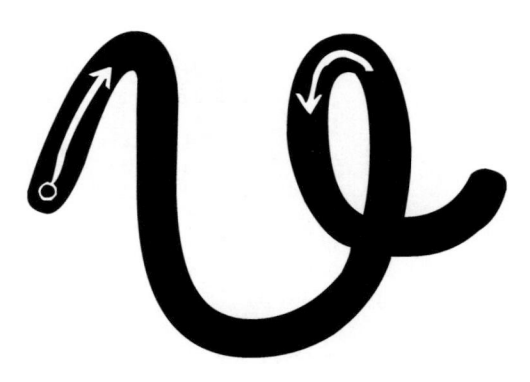

vase *vase* *vase* *vase* *vase*
vase *vase*
vase *vase*
vase *vase*

eleven *eleven* *eleven* *eleven*
eleven *eleven*
eleven *eleven*
eleven *eleven*

vase

eleven

72

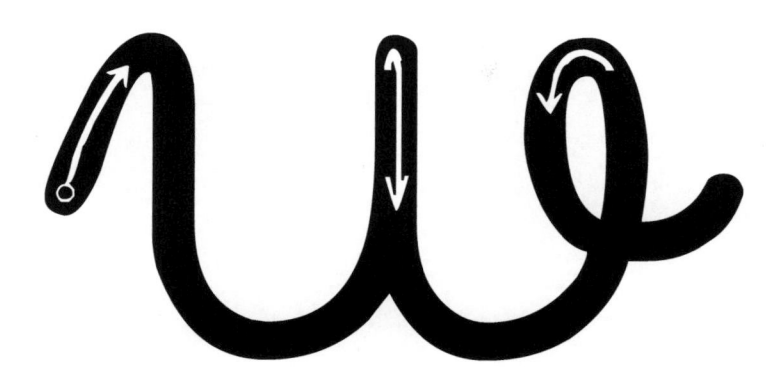

w

wing wing wing wing wing
wing wing
wing wing
wing wing

kiwi kiwi kiwi kiwi kiwi
kiwi kiwi
kiwi kiwi
kiwi kiwi

wing

kiwi

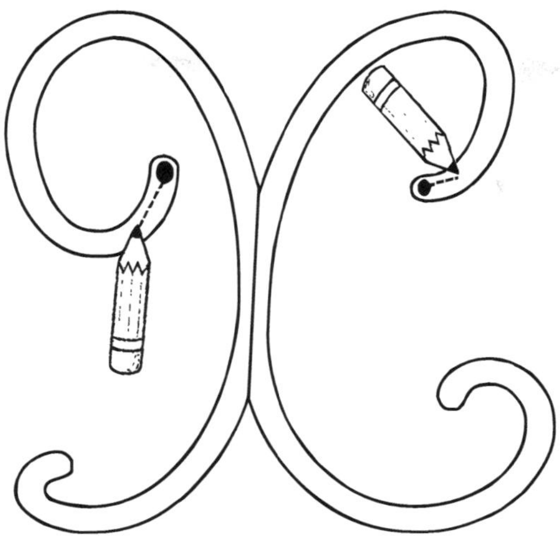

X X X X X X

X X X X X X

X X X X X X

X

X

76

xylophone xylophone xylophone
xylophone xylophone
xylophone xylophone
xylophone xylophone

boxing boxing boxing boxing
boxing boxing
boxing boxing
boxing boxing

xylophone

boxing

78

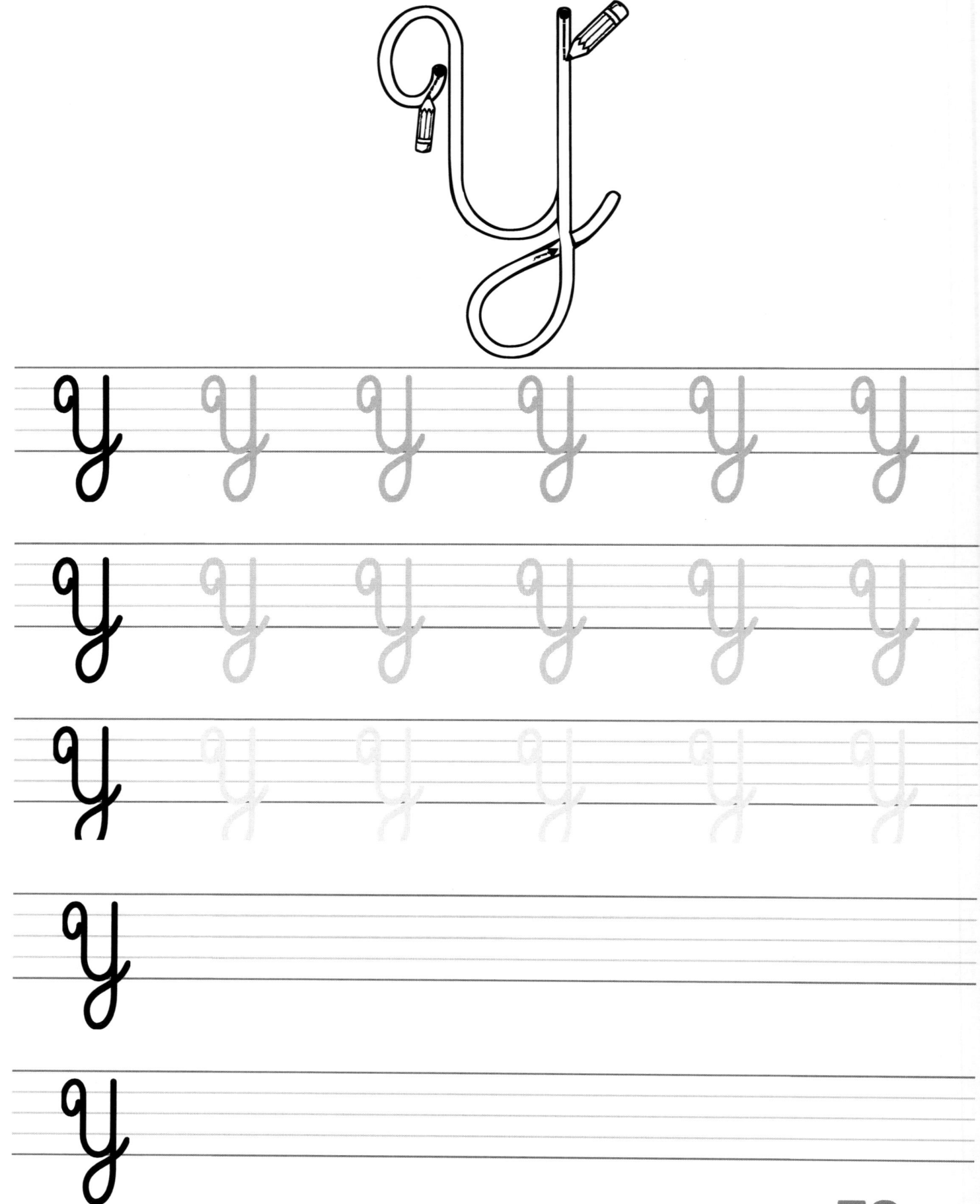

y

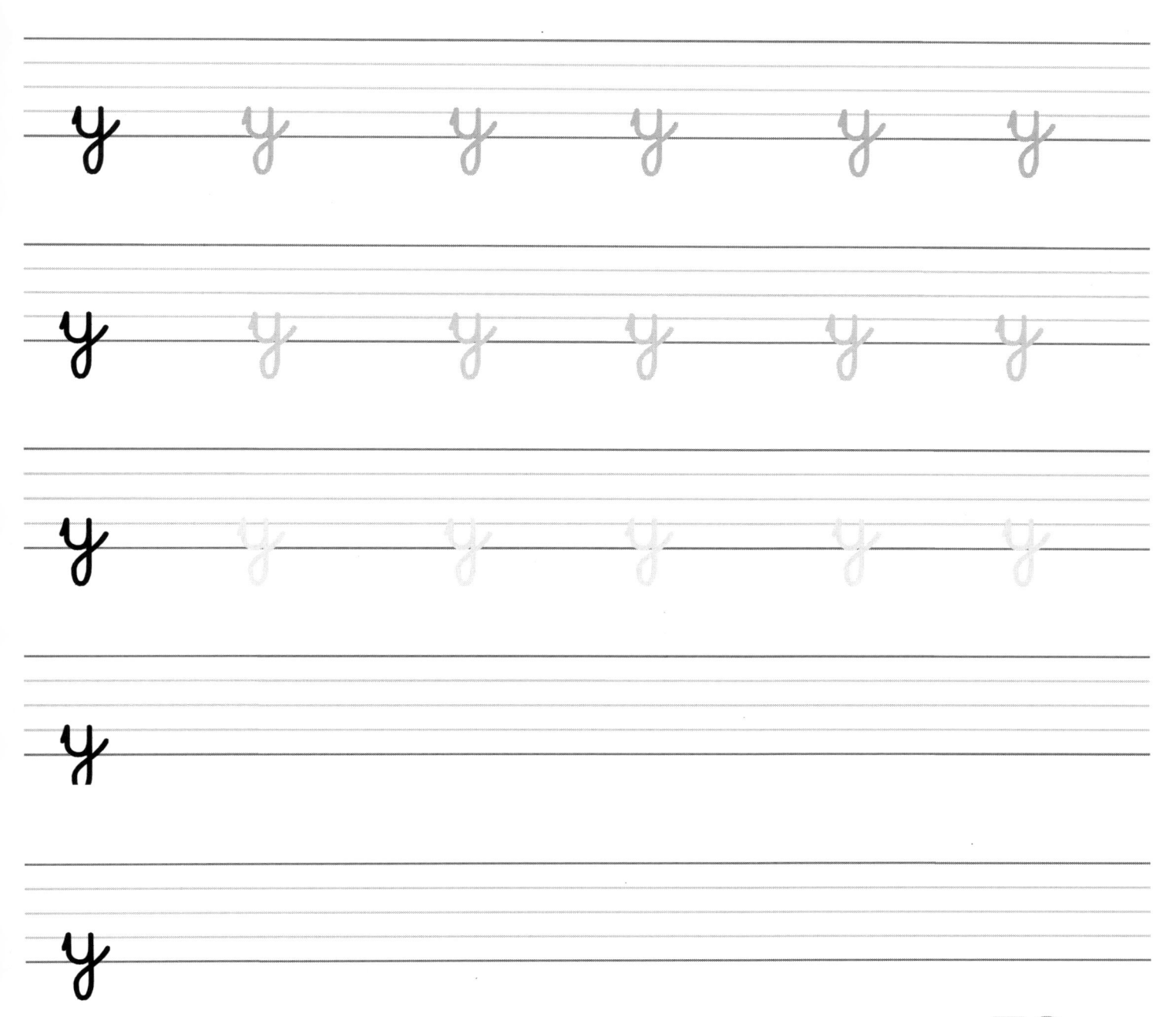

yacht yacht yacht yacht yacht
yacht yacht
yacht yacht
yacht yacht

eye eye eye eye eye eye
eye eye
eye eye
eye eye

yacht

eye

Z

Z Z Z Z Z Z

Z Z Z Z Z Z

Z Z Z Z Z Z

Z

Z

zèbra   zèbra   zèbra   zèbra   zèbra
zèbra   zèbra
zèbra   zèbra
zèbra   zèbra

pizza   pizza   pizza   pizza   pizza
pizza   pizza
pizza   pizza
pizza   pizza

zèbra

pizza

"An eye for an eye will only make the whole world blind."

Mahatma Gandhi

An eye for an eye will only

make the whole world blind

An eye for an eye will only

make the whole world blind

An eye for an eye will only

make the whole world blind

“It is never too late to be what you might have been.”

George Eliot

It is never too late to be

what you might have been

It is never too late to be

what you might have been

It is never too late to be

what you might have been

> "You only live once, but if you do it right, once is enough."
> **Mae West**

You only live once, but if you

do it right, once is enough

> "I have not failed. I've just found 10,000 ways that won't work."
> **Thomas A. Edison**

I have not failed. I've just found

10,000 ways that won't work

> "You only live once, but if you do it right, once is enough."
> **Mae West**

You only live once, but if you

do it right, once is enough

Life is what happens to us while we are making other plans."
Allen Saunders

Life is what happens to us while

we are making other plans

Life is what happens to us while

we are making other plans

Life is what happens to us while

we are making other plans

> "I solemnly swear that I am up to no good."
> **J.K. Rowling**

I solemnly swear that

I am up to no good

I solemnly swear that

I am up to no good

I solemnly swear that

I am up to no good

> "It takes courage to grow up and become who you really are."
> **E.E. Cummings**

It takes courage to grow up

and become who you really are

It takes courage to grow up

and become who you really are

It takes courage to grow up

and become who you really are

> "Always forgive your enemies; nothing annoys them so much."
> **Oscar Wilde**

Always forgive your enemies;

nothing annoys them so much

Always forgive your enemies;

nothing annoys them so much

Always forgive your enemies;

nothing annoys them so much

> "Without music, life would be a mistake."
> **Friedrich Nietzsche**

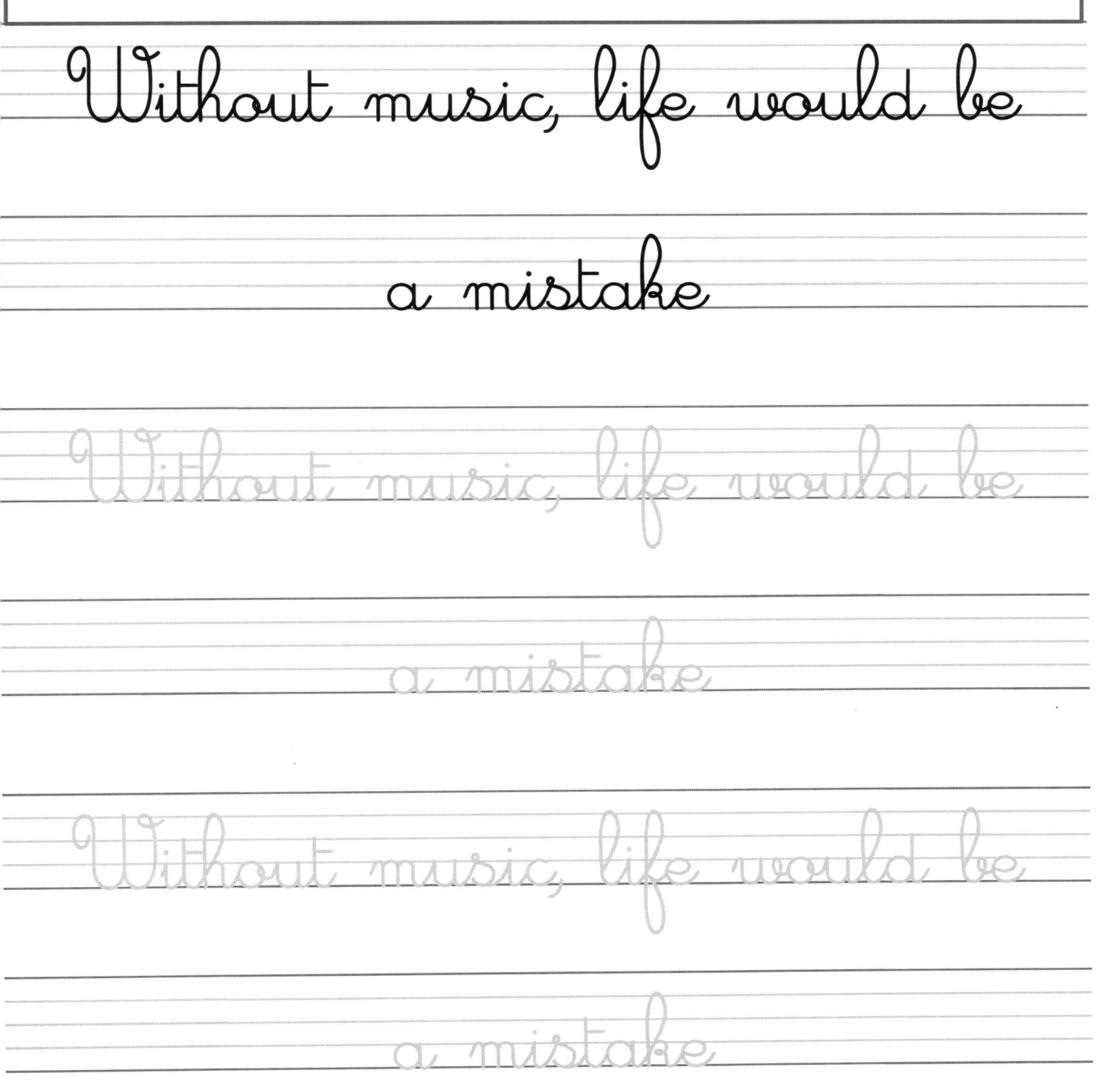

Without music, life would be

a mistake

Without music, life would be

a mistake

Without music, life would be

a mistake

> "No one can make you feel inferior without your consent."
> **Eleanor Roosevelt**

No one can make you feel

inferior without your consent

"Be yourself; everyone else is already taken."
Oscar Wilde

Be yourself; everyone else

is already taken

Be yourself; everyone else

is already taken

Be yourself; everyone else

is already taken

> "If you judge people, you have no time to love them."
> **Mother Teresa**

If you judge people, you have no time to love them

"So many books, so little time."
— **Frank Zappa**

> "If you don't stand for something you will fall for anything."
> **Gordon A. Eadie**

If you don't stand for something

you will fall for anything

> "Love all, trust a few, do wrong to none."
> **William Shakespeare**

Love all, trust a few,

do wrong to none

Love all, trust a few,

do wrong to none

Love all, trust a few,

do wrong to none

> "A room without books is like a body without a soul."
> **Marcus Tullius Cicero**

A room without books is like

a body without a soul

> "I have never let my schooling interfere with my education."
> **Mark Twain**

I have never let my schooling

interfere with my education

> "The future depends on what you do today."
> **Mahatma Gandhi**

The future depends

on what you do today

The future depends

on what you do today

The future depends

on what you do today

> "Everything you can imagine is real."
> — **Pablo Picasso**

Everything you can

imagine is real

Everything you can

imagine is real

Everything you can

imagine is real

> "Be the change that you wish to see in the world."
> **Mahatma Gandhi**

Be the change that you

wish to see in the world

Be the change that you

wish to see in the world

Be the change that you

wish to see in the world

"I am free of all prejudice. I hate everyone equally."

W.C. Fields

I am free of all prejudice.

I hate everyone equally

I am free of all prejudice.

I hate everyone equally

I am free of all prejudice.

I hate everyone equally

> "The past beats inside me like a second heart."
> **John Banville**

The past beats inside me like

a second heart

The journey of a thousand miles starts with a single step

The journey of a thousand miles
starts with a single step

The journey of a thousand miles
starts with a single step
The journey of a thousand miles
starts with a single step

> "Don't cry over someone who wouldn't cry over you."
> Lauren Conrad

Don't cry over someone who

wouldn't cry over you

Don't cry over someone who

wouldn't cry over you

Don't cry over someone who

wouldn't cry over you

> "My thoughts are stars I cannot fathom into constellations."
> **John Green**

My thoughts are stars I cannot fathom into constellations

My thoughts are stars I cannot fathom into constellations

My thoughts are stars I cannot fathom into constellations

"I don't think there is any truth.
There are only points of view."
Allen Ginsberg

I don't think there is any truth.

There are only points of view

I don't think there is any truth.

There are only points of view

I don't think there is any truth.

There are only points of view

"Be awesome! Be a book nut!"
Dr. Seuss

Be awesome! Be a book nut!

> "In the middle of difficulty lies opportunity"
> **Albert Einstein**

In the middle of difficulty

lies opportunity

In the middle of difficulty

lies opportunity

In the middle of difficulty

lies opportunity

> "Go to heaven for the climate and hell for the company."
> **Benjamin Franklin Wade**

Go to heaven for the climate

and hell for the company

Go to heaven for the climate

and hell for the company

Go to heaven for the climate

and hell for the company

> "Threats are the last resort of a man with no vocabulary."
> **Tamora Pierce**

Threats are the last resort of a

man with no vocabulary

Threats are the last resort of a

man with no vocabulary

Threats are the last resort of a

man with no vocabulary

> "I don't know where I'm going, but I'm on my way."
> **Carl Sandburg**

I don't know where I'm going,

but I'm on my way

I don't know where I'm going,

but I'm on my way

I don't know where I'm going,

but I'm on my way

> "Listen to them, the children of the night. What music they make!"
> **Bram Stoker**

Listen to them, the children of

the night. What music they make

> "Our imagination flies -- we are its shadow on the earth."
> **Vladimir Nabokov**

Our imagination flies --

we are its shadow on the earth

> **"Man is the cruelest animal."**
> **Friedrich Nietzsche**

Man is the cruelest animal

"We learn from failure, not from success!"
Bram Stoker

We learn from failure,

not from success!

"It is better to offer no excuse than a bad one."
George Washington

It is better to offer no excuse

than a bad one

> "Scars have the strange power to remind us that our past is real."
> **Cormac McCarthy**

Scars have the strange power to

remind us that our past is real

"There is nothing more deceptive than an obvious fact."
Arthur Conan Doyle

There is nothing more deceptive

than an obvious fact

> "No great mind has ever existed without a touch of madness."
> **Aristotle**

No great mind has ever excisted

without a touch of madness

> "If you want to be happy, be."
> **Tolstoy Leo**

If you want to be happy, be

"Silence is so freaking loud"
Sarah Dessen,

Silence is so freaking loud

> "The way to get started is to quit talking and begin doing."
> **Walt Disney**

The way to get started is to

quit talking and begin doing

> "Five exclamation marks, the sure sign of an insane mind."
> **Terry Pratchett**

Five exclamation marks, the

sure sign of an insane mind

> "Man, when you lose your laugh you lose your footing."
> **Ken Kesey**

Man, when you lose your laugh

you lose your footing

> "Love makes your soul crawl out from its hiding place."
> **Zora Neale Hurston**

Love makes your soul crawl

out from its hiding place

> "True love is usually the most inconvenient kind."
> **Kiera Cass**

True love is usually the most inconvenient kind